Sir Walter Raleigh

Tanya Larkin

The Rosen Publishing Group's
PowerKids Press™
New York

For Antoine

Published in 2001 by The Rosen Publishing Group, Inc.
29 East 21st Street, New York, NY 10010

Photo Credits: Cover and title page, pp. 2, 3, 4, 7, 8 © The Granger Collection; pp. 2, 3, 16 © SuperStock; p. 20 © Art Resource; pp. 4, 5, 7, 11, 15, 20 © North Wind Picture Archives; pp. 12, 19 © CORBIS/Bettmann; p. 23 © Tate Gallery, London/Art Resource, NY.

First Edition

Book Design: Maria E. Melendez and Felicity Erwin

Larkin, Tanya.
     Sir Walter Raleigh / Tanya Larkin.
        p. cm.— (Famous explorers)
     Includes index.
     Summary: This is a biography of the English explorer and courtier who received permission from Queen Elizabeth I to start a colony in America north of the Spanish territories.
     ISBN 0-8239-5558-3 (alk. paper)
     1. Raleigh, Walter, Sir, 1552?-1618—Juvenile literature. 2. Great Britain—Court and courtiers—Biography—Juvenile literature. 3. Explorers—England—Biography—Juvenile literature. [1.Raleigh, Walter, Sir, 1552?-1618. 2. Explorers.] I. Title. II. Series.
     DA86.22.R2 L34 2000
     942.05'5'092—dc21   00-023982
     [B]

Manufactured in the United States of America

Contents

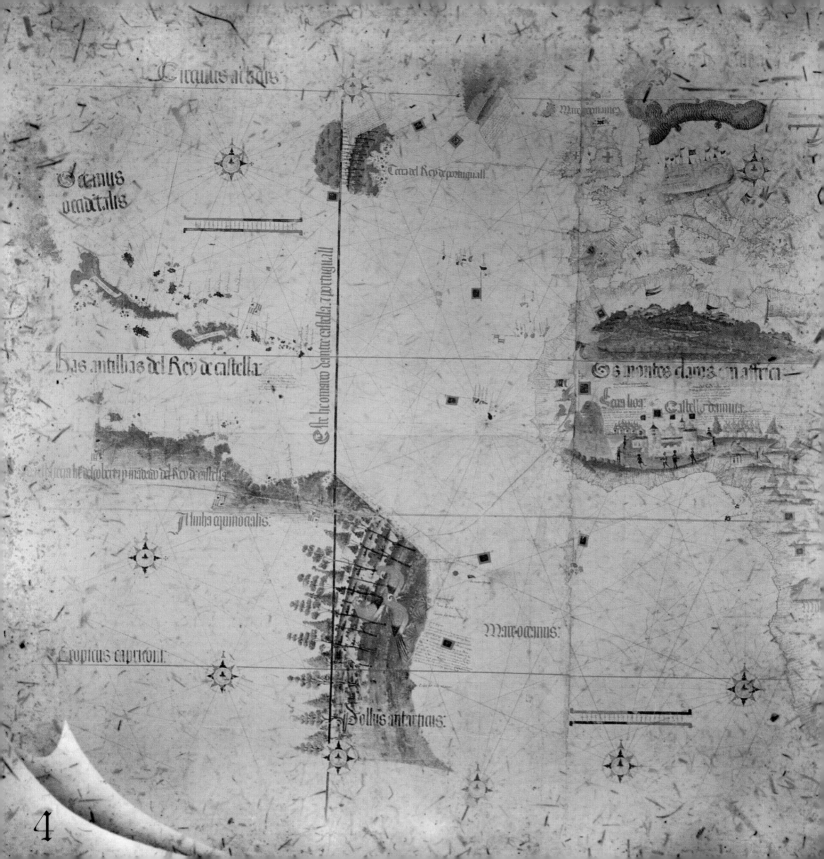

Circulus articus

Oceanus occidentalis

Terra del Rey de portuguall

Mare oceanus

Esthconsano Sentre castella y portuguall

Has antilhas del Rey de castella

Os montes claros em affrica

Lixboa Castello damina

Linha equinocialis

Mare oceanus

Tropicus capricorni

Pollus antartius

4

The Protestants and Catholics Clash

Walter Raleigh was born in the mid-1500s in England. As a boy he had an active imagination and dreamed of strange lands overseas. Raleigh grew up at a time when European Protestants and Catholics did not get along. Raleigh was a Protestant. When he got older, he left his university to help the Protestants fight the Catholics.

Spain and Portugal were Catholic countries. The **pope** gave these countries permission to explore and **colonize** the world. Raleigh was angry that Protestant England was left out. Spain had **colonies** in the West Indies and in Central and South America. The Spanish took silver and gold from the colonies. Raleigh wanted to help England get some of Spain's wealth.

Sir Walter Raleigh (this page) was Protestant and fought against Catholics. Maps from the 1500s showed lands that explorers had reached (left).

Good Connections

Raleigh was poor when he was young, but he had rich relatives. The **navigator** Sir Francis Drake, who sailed around the world, was Raleigh's cousin. Humphrey Gilbert, a seaman, was Raleigh's half brother. Gilbert and Raleigh had a plan. They were going to travel to the New World. They wanted to claim the country of Newfoundland in North America. They also wanted to take the West Indies from the Spanish. The two men left England in 1578. They were attacked by Spanish ships and had to turn back. For the time being, Raleigh had to give up his idea of colonizing parts of the New World. Instead he helped the English fight the Irish Catholics. Raleigh complained to Queen Elizabeth I that the English soldiers weren't doing a good job.

Sir Francis Drake (above) and Humphrey Gilbert (below) were both relatives of Raleigh.

7

8

The Queen's Favorite

Queen Elizabeth I was called the Virgin Queen because she never married. Still, she liked to have smart, handsome men nearby. They praised her and told her jokes. She gave them land, houses, and important jobs. Raleigh became one of the queen's favorite **advisors**. He gave her advice about how to run the country. In return the queen gave Raleigh a palace on the Thames River in England. She also gave him control of the country's wine business and permission to **export** woolen cloth. The queen made Raleigh a **knight** in 1585. Later he became captain of her guard. This meant he was in charge of the soldiers who protected the queen. All these things made him very rich.

Raleigh showed good manners by putting down his coat for Queen Elizabeth I. Raleigh was one of the queen's favorite men.

The Colony of Virginia

Raleigh still wanted to explore the New World. He convinced Queen Elizabeth I to let him start a colony in America north of the Spanish territories. Raleigh told her that he would name the new land Virginia, for the Virgin Queen. Raleigh chose settlers for Virginia who were strong, healthy, and brave.

When they were about to leave England, Queen Elizabeth I made Raleigh stay at court. Raleigh's cousin, Sir Richard Grenville, **commanded** the ships instead. The ships arrived in the New World on Roanoke Island. Then Grenville returned to England. Indians **threatened** to kill the settlers that remained. It was too cold to plant crops, so they ran out of food. The settlers called this the Starving Time.

The sun sets on Roanoke Island, a hard place for settlers.

11

12

The Lost Colony

Luckily, help came to the Roanoke settlers. Raleigh's cousin Sir Francis Drake had been stealing Spanish treasures in the New World. He sailed up to Roanoke. The settlers begged him to take them home. They all left with Drake. When Grenville arrived a few weeks later he found no one there.

Grenville left another 15 settlers in Roanoke. Raleigh signed up more than 100 men and women to go to Roanoke to try again. He promised each man 500 acres of land. When the colonists reached Roanoke in 1587, they learned that the Indians had killed the 15 settlers that Grenville had left. The **governor** of Roanoke went to England to get help. He returned in 1590, but now the colonists that Raleigh had sent had all disappeared.

Raleigh organized expeditions to Roanoke but never set foot there himself.

Prisoner in the Tower

Back in England, Raleigh secretly married Bess Throckmorton. Bess was one of Queen Elizabeth I's maids of honor. The queen did not want Raleigh to get married. She punished Raleigh by locking him and Bess in the Tower. The Tower was once a palace. Later, it became a prison and a place where people were **executed**. Raleigh wrote the queen many poems. He hoped the poems would please her so she would free him and Bess. However, riches convinced her more. Raleigh had **fleets** out searching for gold. One of Raleigh's fleets had returned to England with stolen Spanish treasure. Raleigh gave it to Queen Elizabeth I and she set Raleigh and Bess free.

Raleigh wrote poems to Queen Elizabeth I from the Tower. He hoped that the poems would convince her to free him.

15

16

In Search of a Golden City

When he got out of the Tower, Raleigh became a member of the English **Parliament**. Parliament made the country's laws. Raleigh tried to convince Parliament that England should create colonies in the Americas. He dreamed of finding the golden city in the South American jungle.

In 1595, Raleigh and his men went to a place in South America now called Guyana. An Indian guide led them up the Orinoco River. The sun was hot and trees blocked their way. They kept going. The explorers discovered birds and strange fruit. They named one fruit the pineapple, meaning princess of fruits. Heavy rains finally stopped the explorers. They returned to England without finding the golden city. Raleigh wanted another chance.

The explorers found fruits such as pineapples in South America. They had never seen fruits like these before.

17

James I, the New King

In 1603, Queen Elizabeth I died from a fever. Raleigh was busy fighting the Spanish again. James I from Scotland became the new king of England. He was Catholic. He was angry with Raleigh for fighting other Catholics. King James I wanted England to be at peace with other countries. Queen Elizabeth I's other **courtiers** had come to court to **praise** King James I. Raleigh did not. This made the king angry. The king punished Raleigh by taking away his land and his houses. Raleigh's enemies said he planned to kill the king. They said this without having proof. King James I **charged** Raleigh with **treason** and ordered his death. Right before the execution the king changed his mind. He let Raleigh live.

King James I of England did not like Raleigh. →

19.

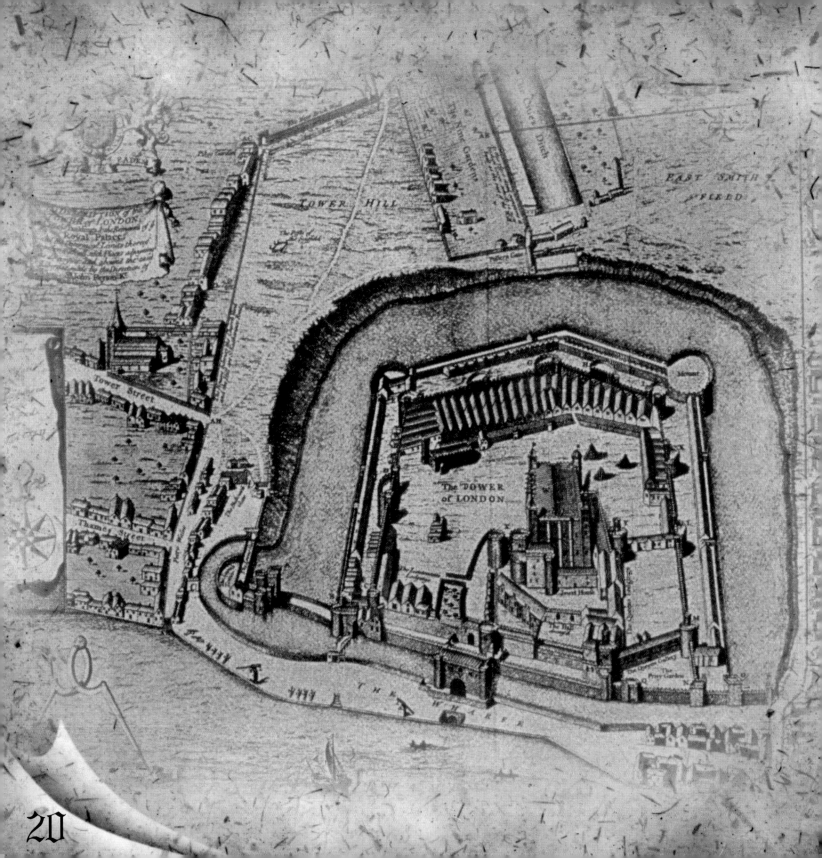

The TOWER of LONDON

TOWER HILL

EAST SMITH FEELD

Tower Street

Thames Street

20

Friendship With Prince Henry

Raleigh was sent to the Tower again. He stayed there for 13 years. Raleigh's wife and son lived there with him. Raleigh had a garden in the Tower. He could grow and study plants. In a **laboratory**, he studied **chemistry**. The king's wife, Queen Anne, and their oldest son, Prince Henry, visited often. Raleigh and Prince Henry loved each other like father and son. Raleigh told the prince about the lands where he had traveled. He told Prince Henry that England could become stronger by creating colonies. Prince Henry had many questions. To answer them, Raleigh wrote a book called *The History of the World.* When Prince Henry died of a fever, Raleigh felt sad and lonely. Losing this friend was like losing a son.

Raleigh studied plants and wrote books while he was in the Tower.

A Renaissance Man

Raleigh was freed in 1616. He promised King James I that he would find gold in Guyana without fighting the Spanish. Raleigh did fight the Spanish, though. In 1618, King James I sentenced Raleigh to death.

During his life, Raleigh accomplished many different things. He was a soldier, seaman, explorer, courtier, and writer.

Sir Walter Raleigh's Timeline

Mid-1500s–Raleigh is born in England.

1590–The Roanoke colony settlers disappear.

1595–Raleigh searches for the city of gold in South America.

1618–Raleigh is sentenced to death.

Glossary

advisors (ad-VYS-ers) People who help you make decisions.

charged (CHARJD) To have accused a person of something.

chemistry (KEH-mih-stree) A type of science.

colonize (KAH-luh-nyz) To set up an area in a new country and have people settle there.

colonies (KAH-lo-neez) Areas in a new country where large groups of people move who are still ruled by the leaders and laws of their old country.

commanded (ko-MAND-ed) To have told someone or something what to do.

courtiers (KORT-ee-yerz) People who are part of a king's or a queen's court.

executed (EK-suh-KYOO-tid) To have been put to death.

export (EKS-port) To send something to another country for trade.

fleets (FLEETS) Many ships under the command of one person.

governor (GUV-vuh-nur) An official that is put in charge of a colony by a king or queen.

knight (NYT) A member of a special group of soldiers.

laboratory (LA-bruh-tor-ee) A room where scientists perform tests.

navigator (NAH-vuh-gay-tur) An explorer of the seas.

Parliament (PAR-lih-mint) The group of people in England who make laws for the country.

pope (POHP) The leader of the Catholic Church.

praise (PRAYZ) To say nice things about someone.

threatened (THREH-tund) To have told a person you will cause him or her harm.

treason (TREE-zun) The crime of planning to kill the king or queen.

Index

Web Sites

To learn more about Sir Walter Raleigh, check out these Web sites:

http://who2.com/sirwalterraleigh.html
http://www.outerbanks-nc.com/manteo/history